… The …

MIND

THE
CONTROL
CENTER
OF YOUR
LIFE

ESE DUKE

ARCHWAY
PUBLISHING

Copyright © 2024 Ese Duke.

All rights reserved. No part of this book may be used or reproduced by any means, graphic, electronic, or mechanical, including photocopying, recording, taping or by any information storage retrieval system without the written permission of the author except in the case of brief quotations embodied in critical articles and reviews.

Archway Publishing books may be ordered through booksellers or by contacting:

Archway Publishing
1663 Liberty Drive
Bloomington, IN 47403
www.archwaypublishing.com
844-669-3957

Because of the dynamic nature of the Internet, any web addresses or links contained in this book may have changed since publication and may no longer be valid. The views expressed in this work are solely those of the author and do not necessarily reflect the views of the publisher, and the publisher hereby disclaims any responsibility for them.

Any people depicted in stock imagery provided by Getty Images are models, and such images are being used for illustrative purposes only.
Certain stock imagery © Getty Images.

All scripture quotations unless otherwise indicated are taken
from the King James Version (KJV) of the Bible.

Scripture quotations marked AMPC are taken from the Amplified Bible, Classic Edition Copyright © 1954, 1958, 1962, 1964, 1965, 1987 by The Lockman Foundation

Scripture quotations marked NIV are taken from the Holy Bible, New International Version®, NIV®. Copyright © 1973, 1978, 1984 by Biblica, Inc.™ Used by permission of Zondervan. All rights reserved worldwide.

Scripture quotations marked NKJV are taken from the New King James Version. Copyright © 1982 by Thomas Nelson, Inc. Used by permission. All rights reserved.

Scripture quotations marked AMP are taken from the Amplified® Bible, Copyright © 1954, 1958, 1962, 1964, 1965, 1987 by The Lockman Foundation. Used by permission.

Scripture quotations marked BSB are taken from The Holy Bible, Berean Study Bible, BSB. Copyright ©2016, 2018 by Bible Hub. Used by Permission. All Rights Reserved Worldwide.

ISBN: 978-1-6657-5581-8 (sc)
ISBN: 978-1-6657-5582-5 (hc)
ISBN: 978-1-6657-5583-2 (e)

Library of Congress Control Number: 2024901906

Print information available on the last page.

Archway Publishing rev. date: 4/9/2024

Dedication

First and foremost, I dedicate this book to the precious Holy Spirit. He is my best friend, senior partner, and my guide who has placed a special anointing and imparted His presence upon my life, which has transformed me forever.

I also dedicate this book to the faithful and committed members of Spirit Temple Bible Church Worldwide for their continual support and encouragement to write this book.

And finally, I dedicate this book to my loving and supportive wife, Reverend Gladys Duke, and to all my children for their understanding and support of my mandate from God.

Contents

Dedication iii
Acknowledgments vii
Introduction ix

Chapter 1   Imagination 1
Chapter 2   Attributes of Imagination 21
Chapter 3   How to Cleanse Your Imagination 39
Chapter 4   Renewing the Mind 61

Conclusion 91
About the Author 93

Acknowledgments

I acknowledge the Father of our Lord Jesus Christ, our King Jesus, and the precious Holy Spirit for the grace to make this book a reality.

Special thanks to all those who contributed their time, resources, and talents in editing and printing this manuscript. Without you, this would not have been a completed masterpiece. May God bless you tremendously and send destiny helpers to every phase of your life's journey. In Jesus's name.

Introduction

Many have succeeded, and many have failed, all because of the faculty called the mind, that is situated between the two ears. If you have a winning mindset, you will win and succeed in life. If you falter in this faculty called the mind, you will fail in life, regardless of how fervently you may pray. You can pray all you want, but if you stumble in your mind, your prayers will amount to nothing. Your mind must be trained to align with the Word of God, and that is precisely what we are going to explore in this book. So, prepare yourself.

It often troubles me when I see Christians who should be walking in victory walking in defeat. It is not because they cannot sing, pray, or attend church; it is because they just do not understand that the faculty of the mind God has bestowed upon us plays a significant role in our human and spiritual existence. I pray that after reading this book, your imagination will align with the Lord's.

If you do not know how to manage your mind and your imagination, you are headed for significant trouble. I pray that you will open your heart and allow the Word of the Lord to minister to you through the Spirit and the Word.

one

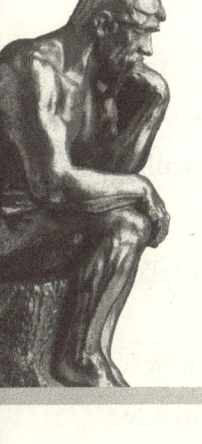

IMAGINATION

Imagination is the ability to form mental images of something that is not yet perceived by the five senses. The mind can construct mental scenes, objects, and events that have not or "cannot" have occurred. You can create what you have not yet seen.

Imagination is a powerful gift from God that allows you to see the unseen. Does that remind you of faith? Learning how to use your imagination correctly is vital to the Christian walk. Hebrews 11:1 defines faith as follows:

> Now faith is the assurance (the confirmation, the title deed) of the things [we] hope for, being the proof of things [we] do not see and the conviction of their reality [faith perceiving as real fact what is not revealed to the senses]. (Hebrews 11:1 AMPC)

The preceding scripture says that faith perceives as real fact what is not yet revealed to the senses. This means faith sees what is not yet seen. Yes, faith sees. Does that mean faith is in the faculty of imagination? Does it imply that for things to actually happen in your life, you have to learn to imagine them as though they have already occurred?

In Mark 11:24, Jesus said, "When you pray, believe that you have received it." This means you need to imagine it is already there. Once you understand how these things work, you will become a master of living.

> Therefore, I tell you, whatever you ask for in prayer, believe that you have received it, and it will be yours. (Mark 11:24 NIV)

The above scripture says, "When you pray, believe that you have received it, and it will be yours." Notice the use of the past tense in the word *"received."*

The AMPC Bible puts it this way:

> For this reason I am telling you, whatever you ask for in prayer, believe (trust and be confident) that it is granted to you, and you will [get it]. (Mark 11:24 AMPC)

Jesus tells us, "When you pray, trust that it is already granted." Again, notice the use of the past tense, this time in the word *"granted."* This verse does not say God is going to give it to you;

THE MIND

no, you've already got it. You are not hoping that you will receive it. You see it in your consciousness as though it is already in your hand. If you can visualize it as such, as Jesus said, then you will obtain it. You must receive it before you can obtain it. The *"receiving"* is in the realm of the spirit, within the faculty of the mind and your imagination.

Do you believe you are destined to succeed? Do you believe you can never fail in life? You have to think as such for it to work. Why do so many people think about failing? Why do so many people imagine vain things? It is because they do not understand the power of imagination. They think they can just think whatever they want. No.

Tell yourself, "I am not going there anymore."

There are places you frequently visit in your mind that are not healthy for your spirit. Don't go there. Nobody will force you to go there. You are the only one who can decide to take that route.

I have to consciously make up my mind to focus on the Lord.

> On my bed I remember you; I think of you through
> the watches of the night. (Psalm 63:6 NIV)

Make up your mind to focus on the Lord, not on the problem, not on the eviction notice, nor the car that was repossessed, and not on your loved one who passed away seven years ago. When you think about the Lord and all He has done, you will feel like dancing.

In 2 Corinthians 10:4, the Bible tells us that the weapons of our warfare are not carnal. This means that there is warfare; something is happening in the realm of the spirit.

You cannot access the spirit realm without involving your mind, because your mind serves as a gateway. It is the platform through which you connect the natural realm with the supernatural realm.

You may be able to quote scripture, but if you do not know how to submit your mind to the things of the Spirit, you will always walk in failure. The things of the Spirit go beyond shouting and screaming.

> For though we walk in the flesh, we do not war after the flesh: (For the weapons of our warfare are not carnal, but mighty through God to the pulling down of strong holds;) Casting down imaginations, and every high thing that exalts itself against the knowledge of God and bringing into captivity every thought to the obedience of Christ. (2 Corinthians 10:3–5)

The scripture says, "The weapons of our warfare are not carnal, but mighty through God for the tearing down of strongholds."

What are these strongholds?

Strongholds are not structures in the air. They are not some armories that the enemy planted somewhere in the sky.

Strongholds are patterns of thinking induced by demonic influences. They take root in your mind and seize control of your

THE MIND

imagination, but they are driven by demonic spirits. If the enemy can gain control of your thought process, he has you in his grasp.

Whoever controls your mind also controls your life. If you allow the devil to dominate your mind, he will inevitably control your life. You can choose whether to believe this or not. However, whomever you surrender your mind to dictates the course of your life.

If you devote your mind to a television program, it will determine the course of your life. For instance, if you spend time watching a cooking channel, you may find yourself purchasing cooking utensils you don't really need because that channel has infiltrated your mind, influencing you to think about cooking.

Through imagination, you can create mental images or ideas that do not yet exist and bring them into reality. Imagination is closely tied to the mind, serving as the gateway to your spirit. In this context, the mind is synonymous with the soul.

> Now may the God of peace Himself sanctify you completely; and may your whole spirit, soul, and body be preserved blameless at the coming of our Lord Jesus Christ. (1 Thessalonians 5:23 NKJV)

In the preceding scripture, we see that we are three-part beings comprised of spirit, soul, and body. We are spiritual beings, residing in our physical bodies, and possessing souls. The soul, which is your mind, serves as the control center of your life.

> For the word of God is living and powerful, and sharper than any two-edged sword, piercing even

to the division of soul and spirit, and of joints and marrow, and is a discerner of the thoughts and intents of the heart. (Hebrews 4:12 NKJV)

This scripture supports the fact that we have souls, which are our minds.

God is Spirit, and those who worship Him must worship in spirit and truth. (John 4:24 NKJV)

We know we are made up of a spirit, soul, and body, and from the preceding scripture, we see the fact that we contact God with our spirits.

- Your spirit contacts God.
- Your body contacts the physical world.
- Your soul, which is your mind, is the portal, the gate, or the door through which the spirit interfaces with reality.

Have you come across a homeless, well-educated man with degrees? What would make someone who has everything, and even more than others, live below his capacity? What would make a man or woman who grew up in a culture where everything is available to everyone still not get access to what is available to everyone?

To answer these questions, we must ask ourselves: What are they thinking, and how have their minds been shaped? The answer to these questions can be traced in their way of thinking—the mind.

Our minds can be shaped in various ways, such as through education.

The most effective way to influence people is to change their way of thinking. If you can control their thinking, you can oppress them. When you think less of yourself, you indeed become less in reality.

By following these teachings, your life will change. Others will even notice a visible difference in the outcome of your life. God truly wants us to comprehend how these things work and put them into action. He gives us minds so we can use them as an interface between Him and our realities.

What is your reality? Your reality depends on the interface, not solely on God. If everything were left up to God, Christians would be the richest, healthiest people, the only ones excelling with happy homes and marriages; they would be billionaires, among other things. However, that is not the case. There is another factor at play: the mind.

You can be born again, but if you don't understand how these things work, you can shout "hallelujah" to your grave and still never fulfill your destiny. Why? Because nobody ever taught you that your reality is shaped by your way of thinking and your imagination. Some Christians go to church; they dance and sing, but their lives do not align with the songs they sing because their imaginations are not in line with their future.

> Now faith is the assurance (the confirmation, the title deed) of the things [we] hope for, being the proof of things [we] do not see and the conviction

of their reality [faith perceiving as real fact what is not revealed to the senses]. (Hebrews 11:1 AMPC)

Have you ever hoped for anything in your life? Hope implies a future expectation– something not yet seen. Faith perceives as a real fact what has not yet been revealed to the senses. Faith resides in the faculty of the spirit but interfaces with your mind. Your mind has to know how to work with it.

Imagination is the act or the power of forming images of something not yet present to your senses or never wholly perceived in reality. Imagination can be seen as the creative ability to deal with a problem, even when the problem has not yet manifested, because you have already solved it in your mind.

If you follow this teaching carefully, you will understand how life works and play it like a game of chess. Before you reach a situation, you have already imagined and solved the problem. So, when it arises, it's already resolved. Don't wait until you reach the river to cross it; cross the river before you even get there. You might have been taught in the past that you cross the river when you get there, but that's not the case. You cross it before you arrive; it's all within the faculty of the mind.

The ability to imagine things permeates all aspects of our human existence. Imagination influences everything you do, think about, and create.

You can only create what you can imagine, and you can only live the life you have imagined. If you imagine yourself as a failure, you will become one. If you imagine falling ill one day, it's more likely to happen. If you imagine that nobody will like you in six weeks, that may become your reality. It all depends on your imagination, which leads to dreams, inventions, and success in all professions. Imagination influences everything we do, regardless of what profession we are in. Even as a preacher, you have to imagine things so you can put them into action.

Imagination is directed toward the future. It allows you to envision things you haven't seen yet. If you know how to worry, you know how to imagine. Imagination can lead to positive or negative outcomes.

Imagination is the key to innovation. If you want to create something that no one has ever made before, start imagining. If you can imagine it, it is possible.

In Ephesians 3:20, God says He can do more than you can ever ask or think. So, if you can think of it, it is possible. If you believe you can fly without an aircraft, then it is possible. There is a possibility for whatever you can imagine.

You gravitate toward your most predominant thought or imagination. Why is that? Scripture tells us, "As a man thinketh in his heart, so he becomes" (Proverbs 23:7). If you believe you are going to get in trouble, you are more likely to find yourself in trouble. If you think all the witches and wizards are after you to take your blessings, that is what you will experience. Your imagination attracts things into your sphere of existence, and what you imagine becomes your reality. If you learn and practice this now, you will be amazed at how your life will progress.

When I say I cannot be sick in, some people get upset, but I have to say it because I don't want to be sick. I imagine myself healthy every day. I refuse to use my mind to destroy my life.

Don't use your mind to undermine your glorious destiny. You have the ability to shape your destiny based on what happens in your mind. Success doesn't happen by accident. No one reaches the top by chance. They imagine themselves there, and sooner or later, they see themselves there. Nothing merely happens. If you want peace in your home, imagine peace. But if you want trouble, imagine trouble. Whatever you imagine, you will attract.

Imagination consists of mental images of things in your mind that have not yet happened. Don't discourage your children when they imagine things. Let them explore their imaginations. Their ideas may seem far-fetched, but if you encourage them to imagine wonderful things, they may bring them to life. If they imagine living in a castle, let them. If they say, "When I grow up, I will have a chauffeur and maids serving me." Encourage those thoughts because they can propel their lives in that direction. If they think, "I can't succeed in life" or "My grandfather ended up in prison, so I might end up there someday," something may happen to lead them there, where they have always seen themselves.

Say, "I see myself on top."

What happens in your imagination will profoundly impact the course of your life. Imagination can release the creative power of God into your life because God has gifted you with your mind.

Dreams and imaginations are possibilities, and God bestows them upon you as gifts. As you move forward prophetically, you are capable of handling various imaginations because imagination fosters creativity. You can shape the kind of life you desire; it all begins in your mind. You must think and use your mind to create your life.

Women: don't let any man drive you crazy; you need your mind for the next man.

Men: don't let any woman make you lose your mind; you need your mind for the next wife.

If you lose your mind, you become useless. You require your mind to serve God.

As I write this book, God is speaking to me, and I hear it in my spirit. It flows from my spirit through my mind onto the pages of this book, and then to you. If my mind is in disarray, I cannot think properly, and what I produce may be flawed.

I may love Jesus, but with a faulty mind, everything I do will reflect that flaw.

God designed us to be creative, not just in arts and crafts, but we can all be creative and innovative. Imagination can bring creative elements into your life. Have you ever envisioned yourself living in perfect health? How about being immensely financially blessed?

Sometimes, when you imagine that, the devil tells you not to go there; instead, he steers you away, urging you to imagine being broke.

Imagining good things can be challenging but imagining evil flows easily. Seeing yourself on top demands a great deal of concentration and focus.

If anyone tries to drag you down when you are envisioning yourself at the pinnacle, politely excuse yourself; otherwise, they might hinder your imagination. Visualize yourself at the top through your imagination.

The Bible tells us that we are made in the image of God to have dominion, power, authority, and creativity (Genesis Chapter 1).

God created you as a creator, and you cannot create without imagination. Everything you see in creation began in somebody's mind who thought it out and brought it into reality.

If you can imagine it, God can interpret it. If you can dream it, God can interpret it. Genesis 1:26 tells us we are made in God's image, and God is creative.

> And God said, Let us make man in our image, after our likeness: and let them have dominion over the fish of the sea, and over the fowl of the air, and over the cattle, and over all the earth, and over every creeping thing that creepeth upon the earth. (Genesis 1:26)

God is creative and innovative. We can see this aspect of His nature in the diversity not only within our church, Spirit Temple Bible Church (STBC) but also throughout the entire world. God made us to represent Him; you are His original ambassador. God has endowed us with creativity and given us the ability to innovate and give birth to new ideas and creations.

God does not duplicate His creations; He makes things once and expects us to reproduce them. When I say *"duplicate,"* I mean create the same things. We are the ones tasked with recreating what God has made.

THE MIND

God, as the Creator, made humanity once. It is now our responsibility to create more individuals. God created a tree once; it is up to us to plant more trees. God made us to be creators.

Repeat after me, "I am a creator, and I create with my imagination."

There are two areas in which humans operate with creativity: sexuality and imagination.

❖ Sexual

You have the ability to create new life and the power to raise a person to live for God. Yes, you can raise someone to live for God. Some of you have brought life into this world; you have children. God does not just send children from the sky; He created man one time and left recreation to you.

Say, "I can create life."

Yes, you are a creator. With your creativity, you can solve problems, create new things, subdue, have dominion, and shape things the way God wants them to be.

If you imagine yourself as a pilot and envision flying all over the world, you may end up in aviation school once you maintain that imagination long enough. This is because your imagination acts as your propeller. That means, whatever you aspire to be in life, you can become it, and if you don't, it's your responsibility.

Yes, it's your responsibility if you're not making progress. This is not to criticize anyone but to challenge you.

The fact that you are reading this book indicates your desire to succeed, and the only way to succeed in life is to take personal responsibility. If you depend on others for your success and blame external factors like the color of your skin, the color of your eyes, or the color of your hair, you are setting yourself up for trouble. You'll continue to complain until your last days. If you complain about your circumstances, they will indeed limit you because what you perceive as limitations will genuinely hold you back.

Say, "In the name of Jesus, everything I am is an advantage to my success."

Everything you are is an advantage to your destiny. If you are short, it is an advantage; if you are tall, it is an advantage; if you have hair, it is an advantage; if you are Black, it is an advantage; if you are white, it is an advantage; if you have blonde hair, it is an advantage; if you have black hair, it is an advantage; if you look pretty, it is an advantage; if you are not as pretty, it is an advantage. If you can imagine it that way and stop viewing yourself as a limitation to where you need to be, you will excel in life.

Stop blaming others for you not succeeding. If you are not succeeding, it is your responsibility.

I know that some people may not like hearing this, but I thank God for sending people who need to hear this.

God gave me a message of empowerment, a message that challenges you with where you are, motivating you to move forward. I will not alter the message God gave me just to make you feel good.

No, no, no! You cannot remain where you are. You must make progress, and it all starts with your mind.

Say, "I must make progress."

Some cultures may talk down on you making you feel beatable, depressed, and less than who you are as a child of God, but God says you are unbeatable. You cannot be defeated. In the name of Jesus!

Say, "I am not proving anything to anybody. I am who God says I am. I can do what God says I can do. Nobody can stop me. Nobody can limit me. I am a champion. I think like a champion. I live life like a champion; therefore, I am taking over."

That's right. It is all in your imagination. Sometimes, I receive calls from people who express a desire to give up. However, after a few minutes of talking to them, their mindsets begin to shift, and they start believing in themselves again. They begin to envision a brighter future. I work with them to change their thought patterns.

If you imagine failure, you will fail. See yourself beyond the challenges you face. Thinking excessively about a problem will keep you down. Imagine where you are headed. Focus on your destination. Concentrate on what you want to see, not just what is before you. If what you are seeing is not what you desire, change it. Focus on your expectations, not on your experience, especially when your experience is not good.

Say, "In the name of Jesus, I am going higher. In the name of Jesus, I have dominion, I can create new things. New ideas, come into my mind. I have the mind of Christ. I am thinking great things. I am thinking of victory. I am thinking of success. In the name of Jesus."

God gives ideas as you choose to imagine. I learned this decades ago, and it works in any culture. In Matthew 6:34, Jesus said, "Take no thought." That means you can choose what you want to think about.

Say, "I can choose what I want to think about."

Man's imagination is a battlefield. The warfare is not in the sky. Some people try to fight devils up there. No, the warfare is between your two ears. It is in your mind.

You may be thinking, "They don't like me. Every time I go past them, nobody hugs me." If you imagine this for so long, it will start affecting your body in such a way that the next time you go past them, you will start walking with your head down. This will also affect your behavior because what you think affects how you live, how you walk, and how you carry yourself. Instead of thinking they don't like you, choose to think, "I am loved. I am liked. I am lovable." If you do this, suddenly, you will start walking with your head up.

THE MIND

Say, "I am a champion. Men and women look up to me. Therefore, I must do things right."

Whatever action you display affects those around you. It is not just you and God but you and everybody. When you look at things in that way, it changes your behavior. Things begin to change because your thoughts are in line with the life God has destined for you to live.

> For though we walk in the flesh, we do not war after the flesh: for the weapons of our warfare are not carnal, but mighty through God to the pulling down of strong holds; casting down imaginations, and every high thing that exalteth itself against the knowledge of God, and bringing into captivity every thought to the obedience of Christ. (2 Corinthians 10:3–5)

Where is the warfare? Is it in the sky? Where is God? God is inside you; He lives in you. He is very close to you, closer than your spouse or your best friend.

The warfare is in your mind, and God is in your spirit. You have physical realities that happen as a result of how you deal with the warfare in your mind. The spirit cannot manifest if the mind is not cooperating. Your spirit cannot manifest realities if your mind is not lined up with God's Word. Let's look at the same scripture in the NIV rendering:

> For though we live in the world, we do not wage war as the world does. The weapons we fight with are not the weapons of the world. On the contrary, they have divine power to demolish strongholds. We demolish arguments and every pretension that sets itself up against the knowledge of God, and we take captive every thought to make it obedient to Christ. (2 Corinthians 10:3–5 NIV)

Imaginations can exalt themselves against the knowledge of God. So, cast down every imagination that tries to exalt itself above God's knowledge. In Romans 12:2, the Bible tells us to subject our minds to God's Word.

Stop wasting your time trying to bind the devil while your mind is wandering everywhere. How can you imagine failure and trouble while you are busy binding the devil? Bind your mind to God's Word and see how things begin to change drastically in your life. When God speaks, He speaks to your spirit and it enters your mind as images, impressions, or new ideas you never knew were possible.

The devil speaks from the outside. He speaks to your imaginations and feelings. They also enter your mind as images and impressions or words, and they can become fantasies and bring you into a place of bondage.

The devil enters your mind through your imagination, not your born-again spirit. When he is not properly managed, the course of your life can be directly affected. The battlefield is in your mind. Imaginations are in your mind, so from now on, you have to decide what you are going to imagine. Nobody does anything without first thinking about it. You can arrest your thoughts if you know how to cast down imaginations that are not in line with God's Word. You have the power to imagine in line with God's Word.

Say, "My imagination will be used to the advantage of my destiny. In the name of Jesus."

two

ATTRIBUTES OF IMAGINATION

❖ Imagination Has a Voice

Imaginations talk to us. You can choose to follow or discard the voice of your imagination. I have often heard people say, "I heard this voice in my head." Have you ever experienced that? If so, it is the voice of your imagination. It talks to you. In Jeremiah 7:24, the Bible tells us:

> But they hearkened not, nor inclined their ear, but walked in the counsels and in the imagination of their evil heart, and went backward, and not forward. (Jeremiah 7:24)

Anytime you follow imaginations that are not of God, you always go backward and not forward. Demonic imaginations will talk and take you where you do not want to go. Many people have given themselves over to demonic imaginations and ended up in places they never really intended.

Say, "I have the mind of Christ."

When you listen to God's voice and imagine it, you move forward. When you imagine God speaking to you through His Word, you progress. The Bible says they "walked in the counsels and in the imagination." Although imagination is not real, it can manipulate and control you.

Vain imaginations oppose the Word of God and God's plan for you. They never lead you closer to God; instead, they always move you away from Him. You will always end up moving in the direction of your imagination. I often put it this way: you gravitate toward your most dominant thought. You gravitate toward what you are imagining.

What stays longer in your mind ends up becoming your reality. If you know this, why dwell on something that never takes you anywhere? Why spend hours upon hours thinking about something that always leads you to the same place of destruction? The last time you visited that destination, you experienced depression and heartache. Why do you keep going there? Why go to a place that always makes you sad every time you visit? Why listen to the voice of your imagination that makes you think God is not who He says He is? If you follow my teaching, you

THE MIND

will navigate life like a chess game. People will think you are performing magic, but there is no magic; you just know.

Say, "I can think what I want to think about. I choose my thoughts. I can choose what I want to think about. My imagination can be controlled by what I subject my mind to."

Successful men and women choose to think a certain way. They don't just think however they please. They don't simply entertain every thought that comes to their minds. It's okay for a bird to fly over your head, but when it begins to make a nest in your hair, there's a problem.

Thoughts may come, but don't entertain them. They are like birds. Don't let them settle, because they will build a nest and start laying eggs, reproducing and multiplying. Eventually, they will become strongholds, and you will no longer be in control of your destiny because that thought has built a nest in your head, causing you to battle demons that you believe are in the sky, when in fact, they are in your head.

You are trying to cast out the devil in Toronto, yet he is right between your two ears. You are fasting, looking up at the sky, pulling down strongholds when the strongholds are in your mind.

Stop looking up there and cast down every imagination to obey the voice of God. If you do this, you will become a wonder to your generation. What people do to you will no longer make you miserable because you refuse to go down that path. They may call you stupid, but you don't think that way. They may say you won't succeed, but you don't dwell on those thoughts. They may call you nonsense, but you know you are making sense.

You are no longer swayed by what people say, but instead by

what God says, and so you now know how to live life. You are not ignorant of the enemy's devices. You understand the enemy's plan: he wants to steal your joy and your peace. But Jesus said He came so you could have life and have it more abundantly.

> The thief cometh not, but for to steal, and to kill, and to destroy: I am come that they might have life, and that they might have it more abundantly. (John 10:10)

Now, that is the Word of the Lord. Since you know this, don't entertain any thoughts contrary to abundance. God will give you more than you can ever ask or think. So, I am mindful of my thoughts. If thoughts of lack come to my mind, I say, "I am not going there." If sickness enters my thoughts, I reject it. If poverty crosses my mind, I declare, "No, I am no longer living on Barely Making It Boulevard. I have moved to Prosperity Street." When you do this, what the enemy intended for evil can never affect your life. Though he meant it for evil, you are always heading toward good.

❖ Imaginations Are Prophetic

You are the prophet of your own destiny. Yes, you are. This is because imaginations are prophetic. We see that in Jeremiah 23:16:

> This is what the LORD Almighty says: "Do not listen to what the prophets are prophesying to you;

they fill you with false hopes. They speak visions from their own minds, not from the mouth of the LORD. (Jeremiah 23:16 NIV)

Imaginations give birth to reality, forming the future by creating images of your future. How do they accomplish this? When you respond to these mental images by embracing and speaking them, you begin to bring them to fruition. When you embrace your imagination and speak it, it becomes a reality in your world.

Say, "I am always winning, always excelling, and never going backward. I am moving forward, never backward. I am always shining, never having a better yesterday. I will always have a brighter future. My tomorrow shall be better than my yesterday and my today combined. In the name of Jesus."

Imaginations are prophetic, and they give birth to reality. Think about the story of Eve in Genesis 3:1–6. The enemy planted imaginations in her mind that contradicted God's Word.

She was tempted.

In Genesis 3:4, the serpent said to Eve, "You shall not surely die." The serpent challenged God's Word when he told Eve that she would not die. Whenever thoughts that challenge God's Word come to mind, do not entertain them. Entertaining vain imaginations gives birth to undesirable realities because vain imaginations will always oppose the Word of God.

Eve pondered the serpent's challenging words. When somebody tells you, "You will not get well," do not dwell on it.

When somebody tells you, "You will never have a good life," do not meditate on it. When you are told you will live a life of lack, do not brood over it because you will be pondering imaginations that are against the Word of God. 2 Corinthians 10:5 instructs us to cast down every imagination that exalts itself against the knowledge of God. It's just that simple. You don't have to be a rocket scientist to understand this. If it does not align with God's Word, do not dwell on it. Nobody can force you to.

When I received this revelation decades ago, I felt the most liberated. When I understood that nobody can force me to think thoughts I don't want to entertain, I was filled with joy. If I choose not to entertain a thought, it doesn't matter if you present it to me; I won't go there because I know where I want to be. I'm not thinking about sickness, lack, or trouble. I am focused on peace, joy, longevity, prosperity, advancement, an abundance of money, and plenty of good people. I know it works, so I choose to think in this way. I won't dwell on what the enemy tries to plant in my imagination. If you dwell on it long enough, it can become a stronghold—a demonically induced pattern of thinking.

Eve failed to cast down imaginations that exalted themselves against the knowledge of God (as stated in 2 Corinthians 10:5a). Instead, she entered the realm of imagination and contemplated the serpent's challenging words.

Instead of bringing those thoughts into captivity to the obedience of Christ (2 Corinthians 10:5b), she entertained them and began to think, "Really? I will surely not die?"

And when the woman saw that the tree was good for food, and that it was pleasant to the eyes, and a tree to be desired to make one wise, she took of the fruit thereof, and did eat, and gave also unto her husband with her; and he did eat. (Genesis 3:6)

Eve thought about what the devil suggested and imagined it. She dwelled on it and then saw it. How many times have you dwelt on something you know is not good for you? You don't have to think about what is not good for you. You have nothing to lose by not thinking about it. Trust me; you have nothing to lose by not thinking about being sick.

Say, "I am healthy, wealthy, and wise."

When imaginations are spoken, life is given to them. That is how relationships are fractured or broken. Relationships break before they actually break. Yes, that relationship did not break at the time it fell apart. It was already broken before it officially ended. Something was happening in your mind all along, and you did not address it. You kept on accepting it. The devil kept telling you, 'Think about it some more,' and before you knew it, you had words for that imagination, and those words shattered everything. You cannot say what you have not thought.

In Matthew 12:34b, Jesus said, "Out of the abundance of the heart, the mouth speaks." The mouth expresses what you are thinking. Someone might say, "Ouch! I didn't mean to say that." She did not intend to say it, but she did. That shows what was going on in her mind.

Imagination is a tool that can bring you success or failure, depending on how it is used. If used properly, it will bring you success, and if used improperly, it will bring you failure. 2

Corinthians 10:4 says our warfare is not carnal, so that means it is spiritual. We are Word and Spirit people. You are made of the Word of God. You are an offspring of the Word of God, and you are born of the Spirit of God. You are not ordinary. You are the Word of God in flesh. You are an epistle of Christ, and you should be thinking about the Word of God. In Philippians 4:8, the Bible tells us:

Finally, brethren, whatsoever things are true, whatsoever things are honest, whatsoever things are just, whatsoever things are pure, whatsoever things are lovely, whatsoever things are of good report; if there be any virtue, and if there be any praise, think on these things. (Philippians 4:8)

Let this be the foundation of your imagination because God's Word is true, just, pure, lovely, and of good report. Focus on these things. What you speak most often is what manifests most often.

Say, "I am thinking of blessings. I am thinking of favor. In the name of Jesus."

❖ Imaginations Can Be Cultivated

Some people have built their mental faculties on wrong and vain thoughts, which have become strongholds. This can change by cultivating imaginations based on the Word of God. Yes, your imagination can be developed. You can cultivate the ability to see, imagine, and perceive things from God. You can cultivate anything, good or bad. Good imaginations can be cultivated, and so can bad imaginations. You can cultivate the ability to see in the realm of the spirit. You can build yourself up to contemplate the things of God and start witnessing the reality of God's Word manifesting in your life. Nothing happens by accident.

If you want to have a better life, create it right in your heart. Do you want to start a business? Begin a business in your imagination. Visualize your customers ordering goods. Open the shop before you open the shop. Attend school before you attend school. Commence preaching before you start preaching. Initiate healing the sick before you heal the sick. Be a millionaire before you become a millionaire. You cannot think of poverty and expect to win the lottery.

Whatever you desire, think about it long enough until it becomes real to you. I dwelled on the anointing of God that currently operates in my life until it became real to me. I no longer have to beg God; it is like second nature to me. When I am eating, I am in the spirit; when I am talking, I am in the spirit. Even if someone upsets me, I can still maintain my spiritual flow because my mind is so cultivated to live a spiritual life. When you cultivate a lifestyle, it becomes second nature. If you don't believe me, try closing your eyes while eating and attempt to put a spoonful of food in your mouth. I guarantee you won't miss your mouth because your hand is accustomed to it. Your hand knows where your mouth is. Even if there is no light, you won't miss your mouth. Whatever you practice for an extended period becomes your reality in life.

Whatever you focus on most becomes your life. If you think about blessings, they gravitate toward you. If you think about favor, you experience favor. If you focus on joy, you become joyful. Whatever you meditate on becomes your reality. That's how it works.

See with the eyes of your spirit. What you see in the physical realm should not affect you. What you see in the spiritual realm must manifest. Start visualizing health, wealth, joy, and peace, among other things. Whatever captures your imagination will capture your heart. You open your heart and your life to whatever you focus on. As you concentrate on reading this book, you are getting delivered. That stronghold is crumbling. You are ascending higher. You are staying on top. In the name of Jesus.

If you have imaginations that are not of God, you can cast them down. You can uproot all fantasies that are not of God. Do not allow wrong imaginations to linger in your mind and prompt you to engage in undesirable actions. If you don't like what you're doing, examine what you have been thinking. Your actions reflect your imagination.

> From that time Jesus began to preach, and to say, repent: for the kingdom of heaven is at hand. (Matthew 4:17)

If you are a believer and have the wrong imaginations, you need to root them out. Yes, remove them from the roots.

> And it came to pass the same night, that the LORD said unto him, Take thy father's young bullock, even the second bullock of seven years old, and throw down the altar of Baal that thy father hath,

and cut down the grove that is by it: and build an altar unto the LORD thy God upon the top of this rock, in the ordered place, and take the second bullock, and offer a burnt sacrifice with the wood of the grove which thou shalt cut down. (Judges 6:25–26)

If you know that something in your mind always leads you to a place you don't like, you must root it out. Engage in prayer and fasting to expose the root. Sometimes the root of those fantasy imaginations could derive from hurt emotions and belief systems. But I pray that you are delivered. Start replacing those wrong thoughts with the Word of God. You cannot replace thoughts with thoughts. To change your imagination, you must change your words and your perspective.

What are you seeing? What you see is what you think, and what you think becomes what you see. If I want you to think about anything, I will put it right in front of you. The more you see it, the more your mind goes there. If you can change what you see, it will change what you think. Stop looking at the wrong stuff.

What you say has the ability to control and change what you are imagining. Speak God's Word. Stop speaking words that are not of God. Speaking the wrong words will create a downfall that is not meant for you. The devil has come to steal, kill, and destroy (John 10:10). Each time you subscribe to his thinking patterns, which are demonically induced, strongholds form in your mind, and before you know it, you lose the ability to excel in life. But I decree that you are excelling in life.

Replace wrong thoughts with the truth. You might say, "But I have been hearing God's Word, and I can't help it." Make up your mind. You can no longer blame the past. You can change it if you make up your mind. Enough of blaming your father, your mother, your ex, etc.

Enough is enough.

Make up your mind that from now on, you will align your thoughts with the Word of God. Resolve to start thinking right, so you can start living right because wrong thinking leads to wrong living.

Sometimes the wrong belief system will also affect your thinking, which will affect your living. The information you receive and your current situation build up a belief system that can control your imagination. What you believe has a great way of affecting the way you live. If you believe you are of the tribe of the Lion of Judah, no other animal in the jungle can mess with you; you are a lion. If you believe you are an eagle, you fly every time. If you think you are a chicken, then you will be unable to fly because chickens don't fly. Birds of the same feathers flock together. If you show me your friend, I will know if you are a chicken or an eagle.

Don't hang out with friends from church on Sunday, and then with different ones for the rest of the week. If you do, you cannot sustain what you are receiving; because your exposure has a way of affecting your belief system.

Your belief system will affect your imagination, and your

imagination will affect your way of living and determine your destination. In Romans 12:2, the Bible tells us:

> And be not conformed to this world: but be ye transformed by the renewing of your mind, that ye may prove what is that good, and acceptable, and perfect, will of God. (Romans 12:2)

The scripture says, "Be ye transformed by the renewing of your mind." There cannot be transformation without renewal. Information results in transformation. For your life to change, you must have information that will bring about inspiration, leading to renewal, which will then result in transformation, and ultimately, revolution. It all comes from what you put in. God's Word can replace those wrong thoughts, but you have to work on it.

> I will set no wicked thing before mine eyes: I hate the work of them that turn aside; It shall not cleave to me. (Psalm 101:3)

The scripture is telling us not to set any wicked thing before our eyes. Do not look at the bad stuff. Don't set your mind on things that will affect your heart. The scripture also tells us that God does not like it when you turn your mind to things that are not His. So, how do you replace those thoughts? You replace those thoughts by memorizing and imagining scripture. How do you imagine scripture?

❖ How to Imagine Scripture

Let us look at an example using Psalm 23:1, "The LORD is my shepherd; I shall not want." Think on this scripture and imagine it. In your mind, picture a shepherd and imagine the Lord being that Shepherd, and you as the sheep. Yes, imagine the Lord being your Shepherd, your guide.

The scripture goes on to say, "I shall not want." This means, "I shall not struggle for anything. Everything I need is already provided (2 Peter 1:3) because the Lord is my Shepherd. Imagine abundance. Imagine yourself walking in plenty."

Say to yourself, "I shall not want. Yes, the Lord is big, and He is my Shepherd. My life is hidden with Christ in God (Colossians 3:3); I am inside of Christ, and Christ is in God. So, I am protected. No weapon that tries to come against me shall prosper (Isaiah 54:17) because I am inside the Lord, so I am surrounded by the army of God (2 Kings 6:17). Anywhere I go, the army surrounds me. Whatever tries to come against me goes back to the sender (Proverbs 26:27). They may gather, but they will scatter (Isaiah 54:15) because the Lord is my Shepherd. I will not beg for bread. The psalmist said, "I was young, and now I am old, yet I have never seen the righteous forsaken or their seed begging for bread (Psalm 37:25)." I am not forsaken; I will not beg for bread. My seed shall not beg for bread. The Lord is my Shepherd; I shall not want."

Let's look at verse 2 of the same scripture: "He maketh me to lie down in green pastures: He leadeth me beside the still waters" (Psalm 23:2).

THE MIND

Think on this scripture. Imagine it.

Say to yourself, "The Lord lays me down in green pastures. He leads me beside still waters. Everything is calm, no more troubles around me. I am lying down in green pastures. Everything is there. There is no dry season in my life. He leads me beside still waters. There are no crocodiles in the water. I have nothing to fear anymore because the Lord is my Shepherd."

Verse 3: He restoreth my soul: He leadeth me in the paths of righteousness for his name's sake (Psalm 23:3). Think on this scripture. Imagine it.

Say to yourself, "I am righteous. Yes, I am the righteousness of God. I am holy. I am blameless. I may not always be right, but I am righteous. I may not always do the right thing, but I am righteous. Somehow, I am righteous because He leads me in the path of righteousness, not for my sake but for His sake."

Verse 4: "Yea, though I walk through the valley of the shadow of death, I will fear no evil: for thou art with me; Thy rod and thy staff they comfort me" (Psalm 23:4). Meditate on this scripture. Imagine it.

Say to yourself, "Even though I walk through the valley of the shadow of death, I will fear no evil. There is no fear in my life because the Lord is with me and He has not given me the spirit of fear but of power, of love, and of a sound mind (2 Timothy 1:7). His rod and His staff they comfort me. I am comforted by the Lord."

Verse 5: "Thou preparest a table before me in the presence of mine enemies: Thou anointest my head with oil; my cup runneth over" (Psalm 23:5). Concentrate on this scripture.

Imagine it and say out loud, "I know, Oh Lord, that you prepare a table before me in the presence of my enemies. I am not afraid of enemies anymore. They may be around me, but I am on the high table. I can see my cup running over. I can see a surplus in my life. I have more than enough. There is nothing I need that I don't have because the Lord is my shepherd."

Verse 6: Surely goodness and mercy shall follow me all the days of my life: And I will dwell in the house of the LORD forever (Psalm 23:6). Think on this scripture. Imagine it.

Say to yourself, "Surely, everywhere I go the two angels that are assigned to me follow. When I take the right step, that is angel Goodness. When I take the left step, that is angel Mercy. So, goodness and mercy are following me all the days of my life and I will dwell in the house of the Lord forever."

Start imagining scripture. See yourself inside scripture. It is talking to you. The Lord is your Shepherd, you shall not want. Memorize scripture; meditate on it. Renew your mind to become a changed person. As you practice this, you will see your life turning around. You will start seeing things working for your good because you are practicing what you are learning.

The Lord is your Shepherd; dwell on Him and be consumed by His presence. Let nothing trouble your peace again.

THE MIND

Visualize scripture and place yourself within it. What you imagine transforms into your reality. What you imagine becomes your life. What you imagine becomes your experience. What you imagine becomes what you see—the Word of God.

three

HOW TO CLEANSE YOUR IMAGINATION

So many thoughts pass through the mind, and often, you might believe that you cannot control what enters your mind. However, once you learn what I am about to share with you, you will become a master of life. You will consistently succeed in life. While others experience failure, you will be winning because you understand how to navigate the faculties of the soul.

Say, "I am a spirit. I live in a body, and I possess a soul."

> For the weapons of our warfare are not carnal, but mighty through God to the pulling down of strong holds;) casting down imaginations, and every high thing that exalteth itself against the knowledge of

> God, and bringing into captivity every thought to the obedience of Christ. (2 Corinthians 10:4–5)

There is warfare, and it occurs within your mind. Strongholds are patterns of thinking that have been demonically induced. Have you encountered Christians who pray and shout "hallelujah" in church, but when they leave, act in a completely different manner? This happens because they fail to understand that there is a battle unfolding within their minds.

The devil is not interested in your money, your car, or even your house. His target is your words, and he gains access to your words by infiltrating your mind. I often say that your mind serves as the control center of your life. If you can emerge victorious in the warfare within your mind, you will triumph in life. Without a well-functioning mind, you cannot operate with spiritual accuracy. Scripture tells us to be in good health and prosper even as our minds prosper.

> Beloved, I wish above all things that thou mayest prosper and be in health, even as thy soul prospereth. (3 John 1:2)

I often teach that prosperity is a function of your mind. You cannot go beyond the level of your imagination. What you imagine is what happens in your life. 2 Corinthians 10:4–5 clearly tells us there is warfare. That means there is no escape from it. As long as you have a mind, you are in warfare. Whether you are born again, a pastor, an apostle, or a bishop, you are in warfare. Warfare exists regardless of your office.

THE MIND

When you wake up in the morning, there is warfare. When you go to bed at night, there is warfare. When you get to work, there is warfare. We engage in spiritual warfare. However, the truth is, Jesus not only came to set you free or connect you to God, but He has empowered you to have dominion and win the war.

Say, "I am winning the war!"

It is a good thing to win the war over your mind, but very messy if you lose it. God has given you the ability and empowered you to win that warfare that goes on in your mind. There is no escape from warfare.

Say, "There is no escape from the warfare, but I have been empowered to win the warfare in my mind."

People can be casting out demons, but in their minds, they are losing. I believe that when you understand how to cleanse those wrong imaginations, you will always be on top, winning all the time. God made us with the ability to be creative. That means we can create.

Say, "I am a creator because I am a child of a Creator."

You can create through sexual intimacy or imagination. Imagination is the capacity to picture something that is not yet in reality and take steps toward bringing it to reality.

Have you ever imagined being in a particular place and ended up going there? Some people imagine going to church, and they end up going to church. Some imagine staying home and end up staying at home. You can find any reason not to be where you need to be if you imagine it long enough. If you imagine not getting a job, you remain jobless. If you imagine getting cancer, cancer will invade your body. If you imagine winning, you will win. If you imagine succeeding, you will be a success. It's just a matter of time.

God has given you imagination. Imagination is a gift, and it has a voice. Our imaginations speak to us, and we can follow them. In the secular world, this is called self-talk. Vain imaginations are mental images that oppose God's will and purpose for your life.

Say, "God has a plan for my life."

Vain imaginations are thoughts that come to your mind and invade it with images that are contrary to your destiny. If you don't know how to cleanse your imagination from those images, they lead you in the direction of destruction.

Remember, imaginations are prophetic. They give birth to reality. They form a future. When God speaks, an image comes up in your imagination. When the devil speaks, an image comes up in your imagination.

Say, "I have a mind. I can think. In the name of Jesus. I can choose to take a thought or not to take a thought."

Thoughts are the basis of imagination. When thoughts come to your mind, you begin to imagine them. Some people imagine the devil is after them, and they think that all the time. They imagine witches and wizards are after them all the time. They imagine there is a devil in their bedroom. They imagine they are going to hell. They imagine they are going to get sick. They imagine vain things; yet, they are Christians. Since they do not understand how to cleanse their minds from these imaginations, they go through life always imagining vain things and never getting results because the devil got them. I pray the devil cannot get you.

❖ Sources of Imagination

There are three sources of imagination:

1. The Holy Spirit

    When the Holy Spirit brings imaginations or thoughts into your mind, they bring about freedom to operate effectively and prophetically.

    > And it shall come to pass in the last days, saith God, I will pour out of my Spirit upon all flesh: And your sons and your daughters shall prophesy, and your young men shall see visions, And your old men shall dream dreams. (Acts 2:17)

    The Holy Ghost inspires prophetic images in your imagination. He brings images to your mind that unlock your potential, as well as dreams that reveal your possibilities and destiny. Your imagination can be open and yielded to the Holy Spirit or to other forms of imagination.

> For I know the thoughts that I think toward you,
> saith the LORD, thoughts of peace, and not of evil,
> to give you an expected end. (Jeremiah 29:11)

From this scripture, we see that God thinks as well.

Tell yourself, "God is thinking about me."

God says, "The thoughts that I think toward you are thoughts of peace and not of evil, to give you an expected end."

We can also see that any thought that is not good is of the devil. If you can get this, you will walk in victory. Nothing will put you down anymore. If it is not good, it is evil and it is not God. So, if you have evil and hopeless thoughts they are not of the Holy Spirit. It is important to understand this and come out of your current thinking into greater thinking.

Say, "I must come into a greater thinking. In the name of Jesus."

2. Demonic Spirits

These are a source of imagination that consistently leads to bondage.

Whenever your thoughts lead to bondage, limitations, or an "I can't do it" attitude, they are not from God. Any thoughts that oppose God's will are of demonic origin.

THE MIND

Let's consider the example of Eve in the garden of Eden. Many times, we might think that the devil physically appeared and spoke to Eve. However, it's possible that all of this occurred within Eve's mind. Have you ever seen the devil face to face, speaking directly to you? Does the devil approach you in a physical form, saying, "I am the devil. Listen to me"? No, he communicates through your thoughts. If you're not discerning and cautious, you can internalize these thoughts, and they become strongholds in your mind. No, he communicates through your thoughts. If you're not discerning and cautious, you can internalize these thoughts, and they become strongholds in your mind.

The devil introduces bondage into your life through thoughts of gossip, hatred, evil, jealousy, lack, and sickness. All these thoughts are demonically induced. God does not want you to entertain or accept these thoughts because once you start looking at them, taking them in, and allowing them to influence you, a progression occurs. If the devil dangles something in front of your face, don't look at it; don't take it, and certainly, don't consume it.

Ephesians 4:17–18 says,

> You should no longer walk as the rest of the Gentiles walk, in the futility of their mind, having their understanding darkened, being alienated from the life of God, because of the ignorance that

is in them, because of the blindness of their heart. (NKJV)

This scripture tells us that there is a certain way the rest of the Gentiles walk, and we should not walk like that. Do not walk with that wrong, uncontrolled imagination. This leads to fear, anxiety, lust, gossip, and pride.

Have you ever been afraid at some point in your life? The Bible says, "God has not given you the spirit of fear" (2 Timothy 1:7), so where does fear come from? It comes from the devil. Whenever you are afraid of anything in your life, it is not from God. You may be afraid of dying, afraid of Satan, or afraid of witches. That fear is from the devil, not God. Don't entertain the devil's thoughts. Don't dwell on what he tries to put in your mind.

Whenever you have uncontrolled imaginations of anxiety, such thoughts come from the devil; they are not of God. Send them back from whence they came.

I love what Jesus tells us in Matthew 6:25. He says, "Take no thought of what you will eat or drink." That means I can choose what I want to think about. I can refuse to think about what I don't want to think about.

Say, "I can choose my imagination. In the name of Jesus."

3. Your Human Heart

You can also get imaginations through your human heart. The Bible tells us: "Keep thy heart with all diligence; For out of it are the issues of life" (Proverbs 4:23).

The issues of life flow out of your heart, not from your environment or education. This is because what you truly believe in your heart is what manifests. If you believe in abundance, it will manifest.

What do you genuinely believe in your heart? The Bible says, "Out of your heart come the issues of life." If you truly believe that nobody likes you, it will manifest because wherever you go, you carry the sense in your mind that nobody likes you. If you believe it is always your fault, you become a receptacle for blame. Everywhere you go, you will experience blame because you have the consciousness that you are always at fault, that you are always to be blamed, and whatever happens in your life is your fault. That is the devil.

Declare, "I have the mind of Christ."

What resides in your heart determines how you live your life; you must cultivate it in your heart. You have to continually imagine it, live it, dream it, and integrate it into your consciousness. Think abundance! Never entertain thoughts of lack or deficiency. Whatever you visualize, whether in your dreams, desires, or aspirations, will become a reality as you hold it in your heart. God will ensure that what you imagine in your heart comes to fruition.

God desires your success; therefore, He places dreams, Holy Ghost-inspired thoughts, desires, possibilities, and aspirations in your heart so they can come to fruition. As you contemplate these things, your life will begin to align with your imagination.

Through your dreams, you will receive practical steps that will lead you to their realization. Keep on dreaming; you were born to envision and fulfill your destiny. If you are unsure of your destiny, seek the Lord's guidance, and He will reveal to you what you need to do. Whatever the Lord reveals to you, hold it in your heart throughout your life, and you will witness it coming to pass.

Just as dreams, desires, possibilities, and aspirations find their way into your heart, defiled imaginations also infiltrate your heart, originating from the devil.

> For from within, out of the heart of men, proceed evil thoughts, adulteries, fornications, murders.
> (Mark 7:21)

From this scripture, we can see that evil thoughts originate from your heart. These evil thoughts lead to negative events in your life. Some of these thoughts may be a result of past experiences, memories of past hurts, wounds, or painful incidents.

Have you ever encountered past hurts? How about painful experiences or being wounded by someone? Sometimes, these experiences can become the foundation for negative imaginations, and if you are not careful, your heart can bring them to the forefront of your mind, causing you to dwell on them.

Examples of past hurt or painful experiences could include how your father, mother, or grandfather hurt you, or instances of abuse. When such thoughts come to mind and you start obsessing over them, they can become the focal point of your life. They become strongholds that hinder your progress in life, all because of past hurts and painful experiences. You must learn how to cleanse these imaginations and prevent them from festering in your life any longer. You cannot go through life in constant struggle, especially when you are a Christian, just because you don't know how to address these issues. I decree that you must learn how to cleanse your imagination.

Declare, "I must work through it. In the name of Jesus."

Ungodly attitudes and beliefs that you have developed throughout your life also originate from your heart. These attitudes and belief systems serve as the foundation for your imagination, and everything you think is influenced by incorrect beliefs about yourself, life, finances, the devil, and your victory in Christ. Wrong beliefs serve as the basis for imaginations that arise from your heart, but God desires us to experience freedom.

If you find that your mind tends to wander uncontrollably, take steps to regain control. Your mind should be under your control and not allowed to wander. If it wanders, confront those thoughts, bring God's Word into your mind, and discipline it. I understand that this can be a daily battle, but if your mind begins to stray, make it come back.

Tell yourself, "My mind must return."

Have you ever experienced a moment when your mind wandered so far that you lost track of where it went? Has your mind ever drifted into a fantasy world, become so lost in it that you lost touch with reality? When this happens, the devil works against your destiny. The battlefield is in the mind, as we can see in 2 Corinthians 10:4–5:

> For the weapons of our warfare are not carnal but mighty through God for the pulling down of strongholds, casting down imaginations and every high thing that exalts itself against the knowledge of God, and bringing into captivity every thought to the obedience of Christ. (2 Corinthians 10:4–5)

The mind is the battleground, a place of conflict that determines control over your life.

Declare, "My mind is a place of conflict that I must control."

Whoever controls your mind controls your life. If you allow the enemy to control your mind, he will control your life. Effective service to God is impossible unless you learn to conquer futile imaginations. It's crucial to understand that your thoughts are subject to the Word of God, but they can also be influenced by futile imaginations. These vain imaginations must be overcome with spiritual weapons. Let us take another look at 2 Corinthians 10:4–5.

> For the weapons of our warfare are not carnal, but mighty through God to the pulling down of strong holds;) casting down imaginations, and every high thing that exalteth itself against the knowledge of God, and bringing into captivity every thought to the obedience of Christ; (2 Corinthians 10:4–5)

To pull down is to demolish with violence. Demolish those demonically induced thoughts.

The Bible tells us to bring every thought into captivity, not every devil, witch, wizard, or every evil person in your life. Some people are wasting time binding the devil and trying to lock him up. What you need to lock up correctly is your mind.

Don't waste your time trying to bind the devil when your mind is not yet under control. Bring into subjection those demonically induced thoughts that enter your mind. Conquer the thoughts that say you will never make it in life; you need to bring them into subjection. Defeat the thoughts that say you will die young.

The thoughts that claim the devil is after you need to go. Change the thoughts that say this ministry will not allow you to progress. Eliminate the thoughts that suggest someone new will take your position. Defeat the thoughts that come to mind saying, "She is better than me." Any thought that contradicts God, you must bring it under subjection.

Declare, "In the name of Jesus, every thought contrary to God's purpose and plan for my life is subject to me, and I bring it into captivity to the obedience of Christ. In the name of Jesus."

We are aware that we are engaged in spiritual warfare and that we must renew our minds and bring these thoughts under subjection. Imagine if everyone just thought right; the world would be a wonderful place to be. If everyone thought of life, light, joy, and peace, life would be wonderful.

> And be not conformed to this world: but be ye transformed by the renewing of your mind, that ye may prove what is that good, and acceptable, and perfect, will of God. (Romans 12:2)

There is a war, and you must learn how to fight. If you don't know how to fight this war, you will always be on the losing side. People have messed up relationships and lives all because they keep losing that war in their minds. Some people wake up in the morning being controlled by overwhelming negative thoughts that are not of God. So, the question is, how do you cleanse those thoughts?

Have you ever had troubling thoughts in your mind that seem not to go away? These troubling thoughts occur every single day, not just once a month or once a week. You must deal with those thoughts. In a moment, you will learn how to cleanse your imagination so those thoughts may not overtake you.

❖ How Do You Cleanse Your Imagination from Vain Imaginations?

1. Recognize the thoughts

    Recognize the origin of your thoughts. Ask yourself, are they from the Holy Spirit or the devil? Thoughts inspired by the Holy Spirit bring freedom, while those originating from the devil are evil and lead to bondage. The source of such thoughts is an unregenerated human heart.

    You must discern where these thoughts are coming from. If they are not from God, they need to be cleansed so you can live a wholesome life. Life is meant to be enjoyed, not endured. As a Christian, you are meant to savor life, rather than move from one calamity to another. You were created to relish life, but your enjoyment is contingent upon the state of your mind and soul.

    If you cannot control your mind, you cannot control your life. Thoughts wield control over us because we tend to gravitate toward the most dominant ones. What you think about the most is the direction you are headed.

Declare, "I am thinking life. I am thinking light. I am thinking love. I am thinking of prosperity. I am thinking favor. I am thinking increase. In the name of Jesus."

You should know that experiencing these thoughts is not unique to you. Imaginations happen to everyone. The key is how you deal with the thoughts. Do you accept them, or do you cancel them?

2. Respond immediately to confront the thoughts

Do not wait or allow demonically induced thoughts time to linger in your mind. When you recognize thoughts driven by demonic spirits, such as those that bring fear, bondage, lack, or limitation, do not dwell on them.

Thoughts inspired by the Holy Spirit bring freedom, light, peace, joy, and more. If it brings darkness, it is from the devil, for God is light, and in Him, there is no darkness at all (1 John 1:5). If it does not bring peace, it is from the devil. If it suggests sickness, it is from the devil. Anything that is not of God is from the devil, and you must respond immediately.

In 2 Corinthians 10:4, we learned that the weapons of our warfare are mighty through God. This means that faith is involved. Whenever God is involved, faith plays a role, because without faith, it is impossible to walk with God. You cannot serve God without faith. To walk with God, you have to believe that He means what He says. In other words, what He says is what He does (Numbers 23:19 and Isaiah 38:7).

The Father of Abraham, Isaac, and Jacob only works with us through faith. When you refuse to dwell on demonically induced thoughts, you put the enemy where he belongs, and your life becomes easier.

Nobody can force you to dwell on what you don't want to think about. If an evil thought comes to your mind, don't accept it; confront it immediately. If you get a thought that says, 'She doesn't like me,' is that from God? No. So why dwell on such thoughts that originate from the devil? Don't entertain the thought. Don't allow the devil's thoughts to establish strongholds in your mind. Cast them down.

❖ How to Respond to Vain Imaginations

1. You must learn to apply the blood of Jesus to the image

Some people just say, "I apply the blood," but don't really know what they are doing. Let's look at Hebrews 12:24:

> And to the blood of sprinkling that speaks better things than that of Abel. (Hebrews 12:24b NKJV)

Jesus's blood speaks better things and performs greater deeds than Abel's blood. So, the question is, how do you apply the blood of Jesus to the image that comes to your mind?

Have you ever imagined savoring a delicious meal and experienced the taste in your mind? Just as thoughts of enjoying good food arise in your mind, negative thoughts also intrude. These thoughts in your mind often take the form of mental images. The Bible tells us that the blood of Jesus speaks better things. Cleanse those negative mental images with the precious blood of Jesus.

Now, let's do an exercise: Stand up, close your eyes, and imagine yourself sitting in a chair. Now, imagine using blood as an eraser to wipe away something you wrote down in blue ink. When those evil thoughts infiltrate your thoughts, immediately apply the blood to your mind. Use the blood of Jesus to wipe away those images that keep forming in your mind.

Sometimes these images don't go away because you may not know how to remove them from your mind. Wipe off the image from your mind by faith, using the blood of Jesus. By faith, envision the blood as a liquid constantly flowing from the throne of God, and use it to cleanse those thoughts. For instance, if thoughts come to your mind that witches are coming after you, what should you do? Use the blood of Jesus to wipe away those thoughts.

How do you apply the blood of Jesus to an image that is not of God? You apply it mentally because the problem is in the mind. Doing so erases those thoughts that are invading your mind.

In Revelation 12:11, the Bible tells us, "We overcome by the blood of the Lamb." So, mentally paint that blood over those thoughts using the same method through which the images enter your mind. Demolish them by faith, and the images will vanish. Once you apply the blood, the image of the disease will disappear. The image of failure will vanish.

Some people say, 'I apply the blood,' but their minds are still occupied with negative thoughts. They speak with their mouths; yet, the thing that is bothering them still occupies their minds. To erase that thought from your mind, you need to mentally apply the blood to the image of the thought.

2. Speak and declare the Word of God

Declare the truth. Ephesians 6:17 tells us that the sword of the Spirit is the Word of God, which means that the Word of God is your offensive weapon.

Speak God's Word and declare what it says. Speak to the spirit behind these imaginations. Utilize your authority and assert dominion to nullify the oppression of the enemy. Recognize that there is a spirit behind whatever image forms in your mind, and consciously take authority over that spirit. Exercise dominion by commanding it, in the name of Jesus, to depart from your world.

Even if you are born again and consider yourself a prayer warrior, you may still find yourself struggling with negative thoughts. However, by following this teaching, you can gain control over these thoughts.

3. Praise the Lord

   Learn how to praise the Lord in the middle of those thoughts. Praises silence the enemy. I love Psalm 8:2, which says, "You have ordained praises to still the enemy and the avenger."

   > Through the praise of children and infants you have established a stronghold against your enemies, to silence the foe and the avenger. (Psalm 8:2 NIV)

   > You have taught children and infants to tell of your strength, silencing your enemies and all who oppose you. (Psalm 8:2 NLT)

   When the enemy brings thoughts to your mind, begin to praise the Lord. Direct your heart and praises unto the Lord because God has ordained praise to silence the enemy and the avenger. When you are fervent in praising God, it becomes impossible for demonic spirits to approach you.

4. Pray in the Spirit

   Pray in tongues. 1 Corinthians 14:4 says, "Anyone who speaks in tongues builds himself up." Praying in the Spirit not only strengthens you but also safeguards your imagination against the enemy's influence.

5. Redirect your focus

In Matthew 6:22 Jesus said,

> The eye is the lamp of the body. If your eyes are healthy, your whole body will be full of light (Matthew 6:22 NIV).

Redirect your focus and shift your thoughts toward something else by speaking words that counter the direction your mind is headed. When you redirect your focus, those thoughts that have been holding you hostage begin to dissipate, and your thinking undergoes a positive transformation.

Do not allow those thoughts to linger within you longer than necessary. Apply the blood of Jesus; speak the Word of God; praise the Lord; pray in the Spirit and redirect your focus. This appears to be quite simple, and indeed it is. That's why many people hesitate to practice it: because it's so easy. Yes, you can cleanse your imagination and walk in victory. Apply these basic principles to any imagination that is not of God, and you will experience victory in all areas of your life.

Don't be afraid of what is out there in the world. You are not of the world. God has sent you to make a difference in this world. If you can conquer the war in your mind, you win. Some people speak negative words like, "I will never get a good job." When these thoughts linger in your mind for too long, they infiltrate your thinking, and you start going from one struggle to another.

four
RENEWING THE MIND

God has a plan for your life, but until you grow up and mature, you cannot truly experience what He has in store for you. Repeat after me, "I am a spirit. I live in a body, and I possess a soul."

The faculty of the mind is related to the soul. The difference between a baby Christian and a mature Christian is a renewed mind. It doesn't matter how long you have been a Christian; what matters is whether your mind has been renewed. There is nothing wrong with being a baby Christian (when you are new to the things of God), but God wants you to grow up and mature to fulfill His will for your life.

Renewing your mind is a foundational aspect of your spiritual walk, maturity, and journey with God. To walk with God, your mind must be renewed, which means you cannot think the way that you did before you were born again.

It saddens my heart when I see born-again people still thinking the way they did before they got saved. For some, it is a problem because they have not been taught how to think. There is a distinction between what to think and how to think. Once you understand this difference and learn how to think and what to think, it can make a significant difference in mastering life. God wants you to be a master in life, to overcome evil, and not be overcome by evil.

Mastering the art of thinking can lead to greater success in our lives. Your thoughts are influenced by your senses and environment. Knowing what to think is much easier than how to think. When I contemplate what to think, the following scripture comes to mind:

> Finally, brothers, whatever is true, whatever is honorable, whatever is just, whatever is pure, whatever is lovely, whatever is commendable, if there is any excellence, if there is anything worthy of praise, think about these things. (Philippians 4:8 ESV)

In this scripture, we see the prescription for what we should think about. How you think is determined by the quality of questions you ask. Asking the right questions will help you think in the right way. The quality of your thoughts is also determined by the quality of the questions you ask. Asking yourself questions that stimulate your thought process controls how you think. Since you become what you think, the 'how' becomes very important as you ask the right questions and begin to think with the big picture in mind, by seeing the world beyond your own needs, and understanding how this leads to great ideas for solving the issues at hand.

Learn to set aside time to contemplate the issue at hand. Concentrate your thoughts on the subject and the specific question. Delve deeply into all the thoughts and potential scenarios that come to mind in response to the questions asked. Avoid and eliminate distractions by clearing mental clutter. In order to fully realize your potential in your thought process:

- Be realistic and strategic in your thinking
- Be creative, thinking in unique ways and making breakthroughs in your mind
- Be reflective, looking at the past to better understand the future

This is a guide on how to think; however, the most important catalyst for this is the quality of your questions.

> For the weapons of our warfare are not carnal, but mighty through God to the pulling down of strong holds. (2 Corinthians 10:4)

In the preceding scripture, we see that there is warfare. The weapons are mighty through God. Whenever God is involved in anything, faith is required. That means you have to believe.

Say, "I am a believer."

Strongholds are demonically induced patterns of thinking that can affect anyone, even Christians. You can be a bishop and still have strongholds in your mind. Yes, warfare is real, and it takes place in your mind. As a Christian, you may encounter problems in your relationships, home, school, business, or even your finances, and it may not necessarily be the devil coming after you.

I really want you to grasp this concept because if you do, you will always find yourself on the winning side.

The devil is already defeated. He is under your feet. Do you understand this? The devil is not inside your head, on your back, or your chest. He is under your feet, but you must believe it. As said before, anything related to God in the realm of the spirit requires belief and faith. God does not work with us without faith.

> But without faith it is impossible to please him: for he that cometh to God must believe that he is, and that he is a rewarder of them that diligently seek him. (Hebrews 11:6)

With God, you must believe, no matter how you feel.

Say this out loud, "I believe my latter days shall be better than my former days. I believe there will never be a better yesterday for me anymore. I believe it. In the name of Jesus."

The warfare is in the mind, and what controls your mind

controls your life. Vain imaginations release fear, and they can control your mind.

Whenever there is fear, it is a result of vain imaginations. The following are examples of vain imaginations: confusion, self-consciousness, conflict, lust, witchcraft, manipulation, and religious self-importance. Some aspire to be called 'Bishop' so they can feel important, even when they are not, and when somebody forgets to include a title before their names, they become upset. They may call themselves apostles but cannot even demonstrate the calling upon their lives. Yes, you are important, but it is not necessary to let everybody know, "I am very important."

Assumptions and pride are also vain imaginations. When you assume things that do not exist and act upon your assumptions, those are vain imaginations. Being full of pride, thinking you are bigger than who you really are, constitutes a vain imagination. Setting up strategies to manipulate and control others are vain imaginations. As you read this book, you are renewing your mind and learning how to achieve victory over vain imaginations.

❖ How to Have Victory over Vain Imaginations

1. Engage in warfare

    To achieve victory, you must engage in warfare. You must not simply accept whatever thoughts come to your mind. Many Christians love God, but their life experiences often make it seem as if God is not on their side. They act as if they don't even know Jesus. This is because they do not engage in warfare. They passively accept whatever thoughts come to their minds.

Engaging in warfare means you must recognize and confront vain imaginations. If a thought of fear comes to your mind, confront it. If the thought is trying to control or manipulate you, what should you do? Confront it. Always confront vain imaginations. Discipline yourself and scrutinize them in your mind.

2. Renew your mind

To renew your mind is to change the patterns of thinking, the patterns of believing, and the patterns of responding.

❖ How Does Your Mind Work?

You must understand that experiences are stored in the mind as memories. Sometimes these memories become deeply rooted when emotions are attached to them. When these experiences are particularly disturbing, the deeply rooted memories are referred to as trauma. When people experience trauma, they constantly recall what they have been through. The trauma could have been experienced in childhood or as an adult. The voice of trauma can persistently haunt their imagination and hold them back due to the unpleasant circumstances they endured.

We have all faced unpleasant circumstances in our lives, whether as children or adults, or even in our relationships.

THE MIND

These experiences create strong memories in our minds, and the repetition of these memories causes the neurons in our brains to form patterns and become embedded. Whatever happens repeatedly becomes a habit. When an activity becomes a habit, it no longer requires conscious effort; it becomes automatic.

You don't have to think about it; you just do it, for example, tying your shoelaces. You don't think about it; you just do it because you've done it for so long that it's second nature.

Many of us have been conditioned to think in a certain way for so long that we act without even thinking. Have you ever driven to church without really paying attention to what you are doing? Perhaps you were on the phone, not fully focused on driving, and before you knew it, you were at church. This happens because you have taken that route so many times that it has been ingrained in your memory. Your mind operates based on what you have done many times.

So now, the question is, how do you change what you have been doing all your life? How do you change a pattern of thinking that has developed a stronghold on your mind? Some people believe that they cannot change it, because they have thought that way all their lives, and it has become their normal way of thinking.

Whatever you repeatedly do forms a pathway in your brain, making it easier to think or act in accordance with how you have always thought. People who have thought a certain way for a long time often no longer consciously think; they simply act. However, you can change this pattern of thinking by renewing your mind.

❖ Why Do You Need to Renew Your Mind?

1. Renewing your mind with the Word of God will strengthen your spirit.

   > May He grant you out of the riches of His glory, to be strengthened and spiritually energized with power through His Spirit in your inner self, [indwelling your innermost being and personality], so that Christ may dwell in your hearts through your faith. And may you, having been [deeply] rooted and [securely] grounded in love, be fully capable of comprehending with all the saints (God's people) the width and length and height and depth of His love [fully experiencing that amazing, endless love]; and [that you may come] to know [practically, through personal experience] the love of Christ which far surpasses [mere] knowledge [without experience], that you may be filled up [throughout your being] to all the fullness of God [so that you may have the richest experience of God's presence in your lives, completely filled and flooded with God Himself]. (Ephesians 3:16–19 AMP)

   Your spirit man is strengthened as you spend time studying and meditating on the Word of God along with praying in the spirit in other tongues.

THE MIND

2. Renewing your mind helps you fulfill God's will for your life.

> And be not conformed to this world: but be ye transformed by the renewing of your mind, that ye may prove what is that good, and acceptable, and perfect, will of God. (Romans 12:2)

In Amos 3:3 the Bible tells us, "Can two walk together unless they be in agreement?" You must be one with God in your mind to fulfill your destiny.

3. Renewing your mind makes your faith strong.

> So then faith comes by hearing, and hearing by the word of God. (Romans 10:17 NKJV)

4. When your mind is renewed, you learn to think like God then you can actually say, "I have the mind of Christ" because you are thinking like God.

> For who hath known the mind of the Lord, that he may instruct him? But we have the mind of Christ. (1 Corinthians 2:16)

5. When your mind is renewed it helps you keep your eyes on Jesus, even in the middle of the storm.

> Fixing our eyes on Jesus, the pioneer and perfecter of faith. For the joy set before him he endured the cross, scorning its shame, and sat down at the

right hand of the throne of God. Consider him who endured such opposition from sinners, so that you will not grow weary and lose heart. (Hebrews 12:2–3 NIV)

Say, "My mind must be renewed."

❖ What Does the Bible Tell Us About Renewing Our Minds?

Let us look at Romans 12:2

> And be not conformed to this world: but be ye transformed by the renewing of your mind, that ye may prove what is that good, and acceptable, and perfect, will of God. (Romans 12:2)

God is giving us an instruction not to conform to the patterns of this world, but to be transformed by the renewing of our minds so that we may be able to discern His good, acceptable, and perfect will.

To renew means to replace. God wants us to replace our old ways of thinking with the new way. Essentially, this is a form of "brainwashing"– in a positive sense. As you read this book, I am helping you undergo a transformative change in your thinking so you can think differently. When you think differently, you live differently. You need to align your thoughts with God's perspective. The Bible makes it very clear that God's Word

THE MIND

cleanses and renews our minds. Our spirits are already sanctified, but God purifies and renews our minds.

Say, "I am born again; my spirit is saved, my mind is being saved, and my body shall be saved."

Salvation is threefold. If you have accepted Christ as your Lord and Savior, your spirit man is saved, and nothing can change that. You are as righteous as you can be, and righteousness cannot be increased. Your mind is undergoing salvation, which means it is continually being renewed by the Word of God. Your body shall be saved the moment you put on a glorified body when Jesus returns.

In Ephesians 5:26, we see what the Bible says about renewing the mind:

> That he might sanctify and cleanse it with the washing of water by the word (Ephesians 5:26)

Your mind needs to be cleansed. We all require thorough mental cleansing. Your mind serves as the control center of your life, and if you do not know how to manage it, you may encounter difficulties. To discard your old way of thinking, your mind must undergo a cleansing.

People have said the following to me which is an indication of what and how they think:

"I don't belong here."

When I asked why, they said, "Because Brother John did not hug me."

Really? Are you coming to church for Brother John? This is all going on in their minds. It is not the devil. It is a vain imagination. Do not think it.

Another example of vain imaginations that people think is, "I will never have enough money."

Who told you that?

People also say, "No one cares what I feel."

So what? You own your feelings; change them. Some people have been taught that others must care how they feel. Why don't you change your feelings and feel good?

Say, "I feel good."

Learn to always make yourself feel good and be happy. Whenever bad thoughts come to your mind, think of what makes you feel good. There has to be something in your life that makes you feel good.

Say, "I feel good because Jesus loves me."

Some people think, "I am ugly."

Who told you that you are ugly?

Some say, "I am the problem; something is wrong with me."

Others say: "I am too fat." "I am too thin." "I am too short." "I am bad; if people know me, they will reject me."

Somebody came to me and said, "I am so bad, so I will stay with this person because nobody will accept me but this person."

I asked the person, "Who told you that?"

Those are vain imaginations.

Say, "I am accepted in the beloved. I am loved by God. In the name of Jesus."

Some people say, "I should have been a boy" or "I should have been a girl."

No. God made you the way you are. Embrace who you are. You have been made in the image of God. If you were born a man, remain a man. If you were born a woman, remain a woman. Stop allowing those vain imaginations to occupy your thinking.

Sometimes people say, "No matter what I do, it is not good enough."

Have you said that to yourself?

Other vain imaginations are:

- "It must be my fault"
- "I must guard my feelings"
- "If I let anyone in, they will hurt me"

- "Never trust anyone in authority over you because they always take advantage of you"
- "God loves others more than He loves me"

Stop allowing such thoughts to occupy your thinking.

Say "God loves me very much."

I honestly believe and often say, "God loves me, and He has my picture in His wallet." Before He blesses you, He blesses me first. That is just how I believe. You can believe the same if you would like, but I truly believe it.

If your mind is not renewed, you will continue to hold onto these incorrect beliefs, conclusions, assumptions, and blame. Some of us carry these beliefs from our childhood. Maybe your mother told you not to trust men because men are wicked, or not to trust women. These are things you believe, and they form a belief system that affects your walk with God. Your mind must be renewed.

> And be not conformed to this world: but be ye transformed by the renewing of your mind, that ye may prove what is that good, and acceptable, and perfect, will of God. (Romans 12:2)

The word "transform" means to metamorphosize, which implies a total change. The butterfly emerges from a caterpillar, but the butterfly does not resemble the caterpillar. God doesn't want you to remain as you used to be. He wants you to renew your mind or renovate it in terms of how you think, process information, and perceive things of quality.

❖ Steps to Renewing Your Mind

1. Study and apply the Word of God

    This sounds common but some people do not do it.

    > This Book of the Law shall not depart from your mouth, but you shall meditate in it day and night, that you may observe to do according to all that is written in it. For then you will make your way prosperous, and then you will have good success (Joshua 1:8 NKJV).

    The above scripture says you shall meditate on God's Word, day and night– which means all the time. If it's not daytime, it must be nighttime.

    One of the secrets to my success is the revelation of this scripture. Growing up as a child, I didn't have much. My parents were not wealthy, but I didn't realize we were poor until I went to the city.

    As a teenage boy, I read this scripture and had the revelation that if I could just keep God's Word in my mouth and think about it all the time, I would become prosperous. I took this scripture literally and said, 'I will think and talk myself into a prosperous life.' This has been going on for decades. When I look at my life, I thank God that I received this truth early on. God's Word always works. If you never let that Word depart from your mouth and think about it every day, while doing what it says, you will lead a successful life. Let God's Word consume your mind, not your boyfriend or girlfriend.

Think on God's Word, or else you may be carried away by something that is not eternal. When you focus on God's Word, you will experience good success.

Going to church every Sunday is okay, but it is not enough. You must study God's Word. I teach God's Word daily so you have something to shape your thinking. You need to read the Bible, write down in a notebook what the Holy Spirit is telling you, meditate on the Word of God, and use your imagination to bring the stories to life. For example, if you read a story about Jesus Christ rising from the grave, use your imagination to vividly see Him emerging from the grave. Relive it in your consciousness.

Psalm 23:1 says, 'The Lord is my shepherd; I shall not want.' Visualize that scripture in your mind. Picture yourself living a life of abundance, free from want. Ponder it; meditate on it continually until it becomes ingrained in your consciousness. Employ your imagination to see scripture. Hold it in your imagination and embrace the vision. Use your imagination to sense scripture. For instance, in Acts 2:3, the Bible says that on the Day of Pentecost, the Holy Ghost came upon the disciples like tongues of fire. Visualize it and feel it. When you do this, it forms a path in your brain and becomes a habit.

Before I started witnessing miracles in my ministry, I practiced seeing and feeling them. I had to believe that I possessed what would make them happen. When I began ministering to others, what I had visualized in the Word and felt began to manifest.

This principle applies to every area of life. Utilize your imagination to see and feel scripture so that it can manifest in your life.

Declare, "I am healthy, wealthy, and wise. I will never be sick a day in my life. In the name of Jesus, I walk in divine health. The blood of Jesus has made me whole inside and out. My kidneys are healthy; my liver is healthy; my eyes are healthy; my brain is healthy; my muscles are healthy; my tissues are healthy; all my organs are healthy. In the name of Jesus!"

Speak what aligns with biblical truth. Visualize what you are saying and feel it. Visualize prosperity and feel it. See your bank account with seven figures and feel it. Stop feeling poverty. Refrain from seeing sickness. Avoid visualizing and feeling loneliness. Cease imagining vain imaginations, as they can form strongholds. People occasionally experience depression because they have been visualizing and feeling the wrong things for too long.

When you read, study, or hear God's Word, engage with it by seeing and feeling it. In doing so, you create new neurons in your brain. What you consistently visualize and feel forms neural pathways in your brain, and it becomes automatic. Reiterate what you see and feel every day until it establishes a new habit of thinking in your brain.

2. Memorize God's Word

Memorize God's Word, not the television (TV) guide. Some people know what's airing on TV every day but don't know which scripture was read on Sunday. That is lamentable. To renew your mind, you must study God's Word and speak it out loud.

Say, "The Lord is my Shepherd; I shall not want. I am beloved by the Lord. I am loved deeply by God. I am favored by the Lord. No evil will come near my dwelling. In the name of Jesus. My hands are blessed. Whatever I touch is blessed. In the name of Jesus. I have more than enough. Abundance is my portion. I lack nothing. In the name of Jesus!"

3. Control your thoughts

Have you ever had thoughts that you did not like, and they stayed for too long?

In 2 Corinthians 10:5, the Bible tells us to cast down imaginations and every high thing that exalts itself against the knowledge of God.

THE MIND

> Casting down imaginations, and every high thing that exalteth itself against the knowledge of God, and bringing into captivity every thought to the obedience of Christ. (2 Corinthians 10:5)

The Bible does not say to bring into captivity every devil but every thought. You are in control. Bring into captivity every thought that is not in line with God's Word. Don't entertain it.

Say, "I am in control of my thoughts. I can choose my thoughts. In the name of Jesus."

When a thought pops up in your head that you know you shouldn't be thinking about, replace it with a different one by speaking words. You do not replace thoughts with thoughts; you replace thoughts with words. Sometimes when you hear bad news, your initial thought is the worst-case scenario, but if your mind is filled with the Word of God, your thoughts will turn to the promises of God. If the doctor tells you that you have stage 3 cancer, think, and say what the Lord says, "The Lord is my healer."

If a banker tells you that you do not qualify for a mortgage, think about what the Lord says, "All your needs are met." Do not stress and start telling all your friends, "I can't believe this; I was denied the mortgage, and I don't know what to do right now. I have no place to stay."

Our thoughts can get us in trouble. Do not speak your downfall; control your thoughts. When negative thoughts are raging in your mind, you have to replace them with the Word of God. You don't have to entertain every thought that comes to your mind.

Say, "I have the ability and the power to control my thoughts and imaginations, in the name of Jesus.

In Matthew 6:34, Jesus says, "Take no thought." That means you can choose to take a thought or decide not to take a thought. Nobody can force you to think about what you don't want to think about. I want you to understand this so you can experience the kind of life I am teaching, as this is part of the message for a life of ease.

If I only think of joy, prosperity, peace, and happiness and I don't dwell on the troubles that may be around, acting as though I don't even see them, I will continue living a happy life for the rest of my life.

Others may say, "but he is faking." That is their problem. I am thinking right. I am happy; I am not depressed. I go to bed at night and sleep. I am prosperous because my mind is focused on God's Word. I don't dwell on what I see if what I see is not in line with God's Word. I do this every day, and it has become a habit.

When something bad happens, I don't dwell on it because I want to keep my mind focused on the Word of God. I pray that you get this, as it will make you succeed and live without struggles so that no matter what happens around you, you will always be victorious. You have victory in Christ.

4. Be careful what you feed your mind

> Those who live according to the flesh have their minds set on what the flesh desires; but those who live in accordance with the Spirit have their minds set on what the Spirit desires. The mind governed by the flesh is death, but the mind governed by the Spirit is life and peace (Romans 8:5–6 NIV).

When you set your mind on the things of the Spirit (the Holy Spirit), you experience life, peace, abundance, and joy. Conversely, when you set your mind on the flesh, you experience death, fear, calamity, lack, problems, and sickness.

By focusing your mind on the Holy Spirit, your life will continue to shine brighter, no matter what challenges come your way.

If life throws lemons in your path, make some good lemonade.

Don't cry over spilled milk; just milk another cow.

Life goes on. When you center your thoughts on the Holy Spirit, you remain happy and cheerful. You don't just say you are too blessed to be stressed; you truly live it.

Someone might say, "I am stressed. I can't stand her. I am stressed to the limit." The more you say that, the more stress increases. Have you ever said, "I am so angry," and experienced more anger building up the more you said it? If you say, "I am so peaceful," the more you say that, the more peace fills your heart.

Be cautious about what you feed your mind. Avoid watching shows that fill you with fear and disbelief. Do not listen to music that makes you fearful. Refrain from consuming news that makes you depressed. Watch what you feed your mind because what goes in is what comes out. Don't conform to the world's way of thinking but be transformed by the Word of God.

"Renew" means to replace. Therefore, you must replace old habits, old shows, old music, and old TV programs with new ones. If you intend to renew your mind, you must leave the old behind. You cannot continue watching or listening to the same old content and expect your life to improve. It doesn't work that way. You need to change your habits that influence your thinking. This may be challenging for some people, but you have to make a decision. Do you want to experience God and everything He has for you? If you do, you must be willing to let go of things that hinder your deeper connection with Him. I had to choose between following God or going the other way. Life is all about choices; we must all make decisions.

THE MIND

If you want to enjoy God and live a life of ease, you must be willing to let go of the things that trouble your mind. Why watch that movie when you know every time you watch it, you have nightmares? Why take a certain route when you know that every time you go that way you feel sad? Why not change your course? I understand that information is abundant out there, but don't just consume everything that comes your way. Don't read every book available on the market; some may not be beneficial for you. Set your mind on Jesus. Renew your mind by consuming the right material.

What is the nourishment for your mind?

You feed your mind through what you see, hear, or touch. When you watch movies, you are feeding your mind. If you are reading a book, you are feeding your mind. When you read your Bible, you are feeding your mind. Even when you are simply looking at images, you are feeding your mind.

Make sure you exercise control over your ear gate and your eye gate. Your eyes, ears, and mouth serve as gateways to your mind. If you know how to control what you say, what you hear, and what you see, you can control your life. Access to your mind is primarily through your eyes, ears, and mouth. Therefore, be mindful of what you say, what you hear, and what you see because they all contribute to the formation of images in your mind, and these images influence how your spirit receives from God.

5. Speak the Word of God at all times

In John 6:63b Jesus said, "The words that I speak unto you, they are spirit, and they are life."

Another way to renew your mind is to speak God's Word at all times. Just keep speaking it consistently. The words I speak are mine, and the ones you speak are yours. When I ask you to repeat after me, it is because I want you to claim those words as your own. Make the Word your own. When I say, "The Lord is my Shepherd; I shall not want," that's for me. You have to say it as well to make it yours. Use your tongue to shape your destiny.

Say, "The Lord is my Shepherd; I shall not want. In the name of Jesus, no weapon formed against me shall prosper. Any tongue that rises against me in judgment, I condemn. In Jesus's name. Amen!"

Use your tongue to renew your mind by speaking the Word of God.

> Let us hold fast the profession of our faith without wavering; (for he is faithful that promised;) (Hebrews 10:23)

You must hold on to your confession.

Say, "I am healed. I am blessed. I am favored. In the name of Jesus."

THE MIND

If you say you are healed and suddenly you start feeling sick, what do you say? You say, "I am healed." What if the sickness keeps getting worse? Keep on saying, "I am healed."

That is what holding onto your confession is. You may not see it yet, but you believe it is already done. Hence, in Mark 11:24b Jesus says,

> Whatever things you ask when you pray, believe that you receive them, and you will have them.
> (Mark 11:24 NKJV)

So, when you pray, believe you have received, and then you will have it. You don't have to see to say. When you say it, you will see it because you can only possess what you confess. If you speak God's Word over your life, what you say is what you see.

Confess your faith without wavering. It does not matter what everybody else believes. Believe in the Word of God without hesitation. No shaking. It doesn't matter how you feel; do not waver in your confession. Trust me when I say this for sure: I am living what I am teaching, and the enemy cannot mess with my body. Even if he tries, he will fail. Does the enemy attempt to make me feel a headache? Yes, he does, and I say, 'No way, not me!' I will not lie down and say, 'This headache is about to kill me.' No way, who is it going to kill? I conquer the headache. Defeat the headache. Don't let what is trying to attack you become your death sentence. You attack it.

You must renew your mind by using your tongue to saturate your mind with the Word of God until the truth takes root and produces fruit in your life.

6. You must develop a strong relationship with God

> Draw near to God and He will draw near to you. Cleanse your hands, you sinners; and purify your hearts, you double-minded. (James 4:8 NKJV)

Who draws first? You do. How do you draw near to somebody? By spending time with them.

Spend time with God; talk to Him. Know what He likes, how He acts, and why He says the things He says. This only happens when you spend more time with Him. The more time you spend with God, the more your mind is focused on Him. Whoever you spend more time with appears to influence your mind. So, watch your friends. 1 Corinthians 15:33b says, "Bad company corrupts good character."

> Do not be deceived: "Bad company corrupts good character." (1 Corinthians 15:33 BSB)

If you have bad company, it will corrupt you. If you spend time with God, it will make you better. Your mind will be renewed. So, spend time with God by going to church every Sunday, being at Bible study, fellowshipping with your fellow brothers and sisters, and, for this ministry, listening to the

THE MIND

Golden Nuggets, Monday through Friday. Let your mind be consumed with the Word of God.

One might say, "Pastor does not understand. I have a job." No, I understand. God must come first in your life. Nothing can help you renew your mind more than a strong relationship with God. When you get to know God and spend time with Him, your mind gets renewed. Whoever you spend time with leaves an impression on you. The more time you spend with God and put into practice what I have just shared with you, the more you will see your mind heading in the right direction. This way, you are no longer vulnerable to vain imaginations.

It's not about age or how long you have been born again; it's about applying God's Word. You may have been born again twenty years ago; that does not matter. You can be born again today and believe in God's Word, and it will work for you, even more than for those who were born again fifteen years ago, and their lives are still in shambles. What is the proof that God lives in you? When your life is in order. What is the proof that things are still going wrong? When you have not renewed your mind yet and it goes everywhere. I pray that you practice this in Jesus's name!

Let's look at Matthew 12:24:

> Now when the Pharisees heard it, they said, "This fellow does not cast out demons except by Beelzebub, the ruler of the demons. (Matthew 12:24 NKJV)

The Pharisees accused Jesus of casting out demons by the power of Beelzebub, the Lord of the Flies. If you want to change a particular habit that has been influenced by demonic spirits, there is something you need to do for forty days. You might be wondering why forty days? This is because the lifespan of flies is approximately forty days.

If you confront any demonic spirit with the approach we have just shared and consistently practice it for forty days, new neurons will form in your brain, and you will overcome the influence of those Beelzebub spirits.

How many days did Jesus Christ fast?

Forty days.

How many days was Moses in the wilderness?

Forty days.

Forty days has significance.

❖ How to Break Any Habit or Your Ways of Thinking

1. For forty days, practice what we have learned in this book

    The lifespan of demon spirits that attempt to infiltrate your mind is approximately forty days. Therefore, breaking free from a habit requires a commitment to doing something contrary to that habit for a continuous period of forty days.

For forty days, apply God's Word to whatever you are seeking to break in your life, and you will witness transformation. Your mind will be renewed.

2. Make your confession every six hours

You might be wondering why every six hours? This is because flies lay eggs every six hours. Engage in self-confession at least four times a day. Confess God's Word over your life a minimum of four times daily.

The fly, symbolizing the devil, lays eggs every six hours, so it's essential to ensure that you never go a day without confessing God's Word over your life.

You must learn how things work, as this will help you live a life that aligns with God's Word, preventing strongholds from controlling you. Instead, you should cast them down. For some, it may take a while to cast down those imaginations from the mind but do not give up. Renew your mind with the Word of God, and you will find yourself consistently living a victorious life.

Say, "I am a success. I am a victor. I am an overcomer. I am a champion. In the name of Jesus."

Say, "My eyes, my mind, my ears, and my mouth will align with the Word of God. I will reject any thought that comes to my mind that is not in line with the Word of God. In the name of Jesus. Amen!"

I urge you to believe this teaching and put it into practice. It's easy. You can do it. In Jesus's name. God bless you!

I speak freedom into your soul. I declare that from today, you will have control over what goes on in your mind. You will no longer be caught off guard by what the enemy is trying to do to your destiny. Whatever seed the enemy sows in your mind, you will uproot it in the name of Jesus. I decree that your victory is assured — victory over vain imaginations and a faulty mindset. In the name of Jesus.

Place your hand over your head and repeat after me: "My head is blessed. My mind is blessed. I have the mind of Christ. In the name of Jesus. My mind is devoted to Jesus! My mind is for life. My mind is for light, and my mind is for love. In the name of Jesus. No darkness, no death, no hatred, only life, love, and light are in my thoughts. In the name of Jesus! I am victorious. In the name of Jesus. I am winning in my mind; therefore, I win in life. Shout "Amen"!

Conclusion

What do you want to do with this information you have received? If you have not yet accepted the free gift of forgiveness and eternal life that Jesus offers, you cannot experience the peace, joy, and abundance that come with having the mind of Christ. You can accept that gift right now by repeating this simple prayer:

Dear Father, I come to You right now as a person who needs Jesus in my life. Thank You, Jesus, for dying for all my sins. I accept the gift of forgiveness and eternal life that You offer. I confess with my mouth that Jesus is Lord, and I believe in my heart that He rose from the dead. Dear Jesus, come into my heart. Be my Lord and my Savior, in Jesus's name, amen.

If you have said this simple prayer, the Bible says in Romans 10:9–10 that you are born again and on your way to living your best life ever. The message on the mind will enable you to experience your best life as you apply the principles enumerated in this book. Your mind is the control center of your life.

I pray that what you have learned from this book will not only help you to walk in victory but also help others walk in the place of victory.

Conclusion

About the Author

Dr. Ese Duke is the founder and the General Overseer of Spirit Temple Bible Church. He is the President of Spiritual Father Apostolic Covering, where he provides spiritual and ministerial covering to leaders, ministries, and churches across the globe. He is also the founder, president, and rector of Spirit Temple Bible College with headquarters based in Bethlehem, PA, USA.

He is a man after God's heart, a dynamic preacher and teacher of God's Word with an apostolic calling. He has made a tremendous impact in the lives of people all across the world, bringing the message of God's amazing love, grace, healing, and prosperity with a mandate from God according to Isaiah 61:1–2.

His ministry is characterized by the teaching of the awesome revelation of God's Word in simplicity and clarity, the move of God's power with tangible proofs of healing, miracles, signs, wonders, accurate word of knowledge, and manifestations of prophetic declaration.

He is happily married to Reverend Gladys Duke, a co-laborer in the ministry and God's vineyard. They are blessed with six lovely and God-honoring children.

The Anointing
The Supernatural Power of God
Apostle Ese Duke

Also Available

The Anointing
The Supernatural Power of God
Apostle Ese Duke

In *The Anointing*, author Apostle Ese Duke offers a reverential look at the anointing of the Holy Spirit, the supernatural power of God that gives believers the ability to fulfill their God-given purpose. Apostle Ese Duke discusses:

- what the anointing is
- how to prepare to receive the anointing
- the levels and dimensions of the anointing
- the laws operating the anointing
- the difference between the anointing within and the anointing upon
- how the anointing functions and grows
- how to release the anointing
- how to keep the anointing flowing and many more impactful, life-changing teachings.

The Anointing presents a look at God's power working in an ordinary man to bring about the supernatural in the lives and affairs of men.

Pick up a copy today at your favorite bookstore!

Hardcover: 9781480870321
Softcover: 9781480870314
E-Book: 9781480870338

The Presence of God
A Supernatural Experience
Ese Duke
ARCHWAY PUBLISHING

Also Available
The Presence of God
A Supernatural Experience
Ese Duke

In *The Presence of God,* author Ese Duke shows you how to engage the supernatural in your humanity and thereby walk and manifest God's presence wherever you are. This guide takes you to a place of supernatural living beyond your imagination, a reality that God desires all of us to experience, yet only a few have and do.

When you understand how to live out of the presence of God, everything becomes easy. In *The Presence of God,* you will learn:

- what God's presence is
- how to live out of His presence, making the realities of the presence of God become manifested in your everyday life
- how to manifest God's presence, even on demand
- how to engage the spirit realm and get results.

Get ready to move to the highest dimension of the supernatural in your life.

Pick up a copy today at your favorite bookstore!

Hardcover: 9781665713108
Softcover: 9781665713092
E-Book: 9781665713085